Recurring
Revenue
Playbook

How to Earn Passive Income on
Amazon with Digital Products

Sophie Howard

Recurring Revenue Playbook

How to Earn Passive Income on Amazon with Digital Products

Sophie Howard

Publisher: Blue Sky Amazon Publishing in partnership with Knowledge Source

© 2023 All rights reserved www.kindlepublishingincome.com

For general information on our products and services, please contact support@knowledge source.com.au

This digital book contains general education about starting an e-commerce business on Amazon. For specialized accounting, tax, legal, or financial advice, please see a qualified professional.

Disclaimer

RECURRING REVENUE PLAYBOOK

How to Earn Passive Income on Amazon with Digital Products

SOPHIE HOWARD

Contents

Welcome   1

1. The Online Opportunity Is Stronger Than Ever Before   3
    The Growth of Ecommerce on a Global Scale
    Now Is the Time to Focus on Ecommerce

2. The Physical Product Conundrum   12
    Selling Products Isn't the Only Way to Create an Income
    Using Amazon

3. Introducing the New Opportunity – Amazon Kindle!   25
    10 Reasons why Selling on Kindle is a Great Idea
    There's a Huge Opportunity Here for You

4. How I Went From $0 to Six Figures With Kindle Direct   39
    Publishing (In Less Than Six Months!)
    The New Idea
    My Results
    Are You Ready to Write Your Own Success Story?

5. The Kindle Basics. And How to Select a Topic to Write   47
    About
    Getting Set Up on Kindle – The Six Steps
    Choosing a Topic to Write About
    The Research Tool That You Can't Do Without

You're All Set Up!

6. The Kindle Income Stream Model   64

    Building Your Model – The Things You Need to Know

FREE WORKSHOP:

Your Kindle eBook Business Made Easy

As a reader of my book, you're clearly someone that takes self-education seriously.

And, that's a wise move – because as Tony Robbins mentor Jim Rohn said:

"Formal education can make you a living. Self- Education can make you a fortune."

It's true – the more you learn, the more you can earn.

Discover how to set up a new potential income stream selling eBooks on Amazon Kindle as quickly and easily as possible.

CLICK HERE TO SECURE YOUR FREE SPOT

Or scan the QR Code

Welcome

Welcome to the Recurring Revenue Playbook! I've written this book because after nine years of being in business myself and running online businesses, I've seen a lot of different models and I've learned a lot of the different ways that lead to success.

I have also made mistakes and learned a lot of lessons along the way. What I now know to be true is that anyone can find their own path to financial freedom, but it won't be the same path for everyone. This book is for anyone who is seeking financial freedom and the path less travelled.

Read on to discover the path to fulfil your dreams and live the life you desire.

As I started raising my young family, priorities were changing. I realized that what I really wanted was more freedom. I resented all that wasted time and office politics.

I was partially motivated by the financial side, to generate a level of income that would allow me the quality of life I wanted to live.

But I also wanted to have other sorts of freedom, such as location independence. I wanted a business I could run from home. I wanted a business that didn't require full-time work.

I thought it must be possible to start something that lets me generate enough income to live really well, but live life on my terms.

When I started out in business myself, I'd worked in the typical 9 to 5 government job. I'd worked for a university in a tech transfer office for nine years and had come through a corporate model, where I completed an MBA and became a general manager.

I was running a team and writing reports for the board while raising investment for projects and reporting back on that investment.

I saw in the corporate world, that there is just a lot of money being spent on projects and deployed very inefficiently. We spent our days in meetings, sitting in an office and commuting to and from that office.

In this book, I want to share with you the ways that you can explore this world of online business and find the track that's right for you.

Based on your skills and personality, there will be different businesses out there that will suit you and be an easier path.

A path of less resistance and a path to financial freedom. I want to help you find the right path in the most efficient way, by giving you an overview and broad understanding of all of the different kinds of online businesses out there.

Then you can pick the right one for you.

Chapter One

The Online Opportunity Is Stronger Than Ever Before

Let's face it... 2020 sucked! It was a year like no other as we dealt with a global pandemic that kept so many of us locked away for huge portions of the year.

And for some of us, the effects stretched much farther than having to stay at home. Hundreds of companies went out of business...

Thousands of people lost their jobs...

And even as I write this, we're not at the end of the pandemic road just yet. Right now, there are many thousands more people who have realised that the "stable" 9-to-5 that they've always worked perhaps isn't as stable as they thought it was.

Now, it's tempting to think that the entire economy has been up-ended by the events of 2020. It's easy to assume that every type of business has felt the pinch.

But that isn't the case!

There is one industry, one niche, that exploded in 2020.

While every other industry faltered, this one niche went from strength to strength. It grew faster than it ever had before. It hit record levels of sales and welcomed millions of new customers into the fold.

What is that niche?

Online selling!

I know what you're thinking...

"Sophie, you teach people how to sell online for a living! Of course, you're going to tell me that it's a growth industry!" Fair enough!

But it's not just me who's saying it.

The stats say it...

Some of the world's biggest brands prove it...

And Amazon puts the cherry on top of the online selling cake.

Let's look at some numbers!

The Growth of Ecommerce on a Global Scale

When I say that ecommerce has grown everywhere, I truly mean everywhere! Let's take the United States as an example.

According to Statista, online sales have played an increasingly significant role in retailing. In 2021, e-commerce accounted for nearly 19 percent of retail sales worldwide. Forecasts indicate that by 2026, the online segment will make up close to a quarter of total global retail sales.

In one year, ecommerce sales almost doubled in the UK!

Now, let's look at the numbers on a global scale:

E-commerce as percentage of total retail sales worldwide from 2015 to 2021, with forecasts from 2022 to 2026

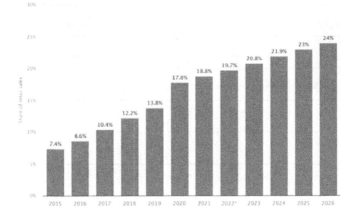

The pandemic may have prompted faster growth. But the industry anticipates that growth will continue when we come out of the other side.

What does that mean for you?

Right now, you have an enormous opportunity sitting right in front of you!

In a world that's still filled with uncertainty, you have the chance to grab onto something real that can lead you to the life of freedom that you've always dreamed of!

Still need more convincing?

What if I told you that some of the world's biggest brands have already clocked onto the fact that ecommerce is the way to go? What if I told you that 2020 brought with it record online sales growth for these companies?

Again, you don't have to take my word for it. The numbers back up every single thing that I'm saying!

L'Oréal's 64.6% Ecommerce Growth

L'Oréal is one of the companies that took a pretty hard hit thanks to the pandemic.

And on the surface, their numbers don't look that great. The company saw sales drop from €14.81 billion ($23.28 billion) to €13.07 billion ($20.55 billion) between 2019 and 2020.

A $3 billion decline doesn't sound all that great.

But when you dig a little deeper, you see that almost all of these losses are linked to sales in physical stores. By contrast, the company's online arm has gone from strength to strength.

L'Oréal posted record ecommerce growth in the first half of 2020.

And when I say "record", I mean they blew their previous sales figures out of the water. The first half of 2020 brought with it a 64.6% boost to the company's ecommerce sales.

And they're not the only ones...

Tesco's 48.5% Online Turnover Increase

For those who don't know, Tesco is one of the UK's largest supermarket chains. As sellers of essential goods, they've been able to stay open when so many other stores have been forced to close.

Maybe that means the company won't see the same sort of boost in online sales that L'Oréal enjoyed?

The numbers say otherwise!

In the first quarter of 2020, Tesco announced an increase to £12.2 billion ($21.44 billion) in sales, which represents 8% growth compared to the first quarter of 2019.

Impressive!

But what's more impressive is just how big a role online sales have played in that growth.

In the same period, the company's online sales jumped up by a staggering 48.5%. That accounts for an extra £2 billion ($3.52 billion) in sales and has pushed Tesco's online grocery business to the point that it now accounts for 16% of the company's total sales.

The number was 9% before the pandemic.

Amazon's Record Growth During the Year 2020

And so, we come to my bread and butter...

Amazon!

If L'Oréal and Tesco impressed you, just wait until you hear this!

In the third quarter of 2020, Amazon announced sales numbers that shattered every record the company had previously set for a quarter.

Revenue shot up by 37% to reach US$96.1 billion...

The previous year saw a revenue of US$70 billion!

And that's not all!

The company's net income jumped from US$2.1 billion to US$6.3 billion during the same period.

That's not just a US$4.2 billion increase, by the way...

That's Amazon's record quarterly profit!

2020 was extremely kind to Amazon. The company has enjoyed enormous profits and increased its employee count by about 400,000 people during the course of the year.

Insider Intelligence forecasts that Amazon's retail ecommerce sales worldwide will reach $746.22 billion in 2023. Net sales increased 15% to $127.1 billion in Q3 2022, up from $110.8 billion in the third quarter of 2021, according to the most recent Amazon quarterly earnings report, released in October of 2022.

So...

What does this mean for you?

Now Is the Time to Focus on Ecommerce

It really is that simple!

When practically every industry has been brought to its knees by the coronavirus pandemic, ecommerce has been able to stand higher than it's ever stood before. Major retailers have seen growth that they could have never anticipated...

Amazon has further established itself as the leading ecommerce platform in the world...

And as for the people who sell on Amazon?

They've grasped an opportunity to create the life they've always wanted to have because they've been able to ride on an enormous wave of growth.

So, I know what you're thinking now...

"Sophie's about to tell me that I need to set up an Amazon store and start selling products?"

Well, I'm always going to tell you that. A great Amazon store is, and always will be, one of the best ways to create a passive income stream that can lead you to the life you've always dreamed about.

But what if you could create another income stream to support your Amazon store?

An income stream that has the potential for five or six returns every single year. An income stream that's relatively cheap to set up has a distinct model to follow, and requires you to have very little technical know-how.

Sounds good, right?

In this book, I'm going to show you what that new income stream looks like, and how to move towards that goal.

But before I do, it's important that we confront some of the challenges that 2020 brought with it.

Chapter Two

The Physical Product Conundrum

After what I've just told you, I know that you're raring to go on Amazon. You want to find that perfect product, create your store, and start taking advantage of the meteoric growth that we're seeing in ecommerce.

That is absolutely something you should do!

There has never been a better time to have an Amazon store. More people shop online today than at any other point in history. And if you have a store with the right products, you stand to make a whole lot of money.

However, I want to make sure you have the full picture before you start your store.

As amazing as 2020 was for Amazon and its sellers, there are also some challenges that the year has brought.

Do these challenges mean you shouldn't start an Amazon store today? No!

The challenges I'm about to discuss have only affected a minority of sellers. And every single one of them is solvable as long as you have the right guidance and support.

The reason I'm discussing these challenges is that I believe in making sure that everybody who listens to me has a choice. If you want an Amazon store to be the first step on your journey to financial freedom, make it happen! I have tons of courses and materials to help you along.

Just know that the following are challenges that you may face in the current online environment...

Challenge #1: Sourcing Products From Overseas

To build a strong Amazon business selling products, you need a reliable manufacturing source for those products.

Unfortunately, that's something that some sellers have found hard to come by during 2020.

Many people who sell products online source their stock from China. They rely on Chinese factories to stay open so they can manufacture the products they sell.

The early months of 2020 saw massive factory closures as China became the first country to enter lockdowns to combat the coronavirus pandemic.

An Amazon seller named Kyle Kirshner felt the effects. He's the owner of Kyndley, which uses Amazon to sell outdoor products. Crucially, Kyle imports 90% of his stock from factories in China.

In February 2020, he perfectly explained why hiccups in the supply line can cause major problems for sellers:

"We're a little worried about that because we are one of the best sellers on Amazon in that category. I contacted my manufacturer today and their factories are closed right now.

"If we don't have product, and we lose our ranking, then nobody can see our product and we won't have any sales."

This sort of problem affected thousands of sellers during the early parts of 2020. The good news is that this issue has all but disappeared in 2021.

The factory closures we saw in early-2020 aren't happening anymore. And by all indications, we're coming out of the other end of the pandemic, which makes them very unlikely to happen again. Still, this is an issue that some faced when selling on Amazon in 2020, so it's worth mentioning here.

Challenge #2: Issues With Logistics (Especially If You're Not Using FBA)

One of the most wonderful things about Amazon is that it offers its Fulfilment by Amazon (FBA) service.

FBA is a Godsend for Amazon sellers.

Amazon handles all of the warehousing and delivery of your products for you. That means all you have to do is pay for storage space and make sure your stock gets to the relevant Fulfilment Centre.

Great!

But what if you're not using FBA?

What if you're maintaining your own warehouse space and handling the transportation of your goods yourself?

That's challenging enough without a global pandemic messing things up!

But with coronavirus having an impact, you may have to deal with a few extra headaches. Transportation companies may not be able to work at full capacity, which slows down your delivery schedules. Warehouses may have to shut down completely if there's an outbreak, which means your stock just sits there while customers who've ordered from you get angry about their goods not arriving on time.

Not good for your brand...

Definitely not good for your bank balance!

But again, this is a solvable challenge.

And FBA, which I've just mentioned, is the most obvious solution. Leave all of the logistical work in the hands of Amazon and there's no reason why this issue should affect your store.

Just be aware that you may have to deal with some minor issues if you're determined to maintain control of your logistical channels.

Challenge #3: FBA Storage Limitations

"Okay," you say to yourself.

"I'll just let Amazon handle all of the logistics for me! The service is right there anyway so I may as well take advantage of it!"

Great move!

However, Amazon FBA isn't perfect, especially during the pandemic. In particular, Amazon has placed storage limitations on sellers that could prevent your store from growing to its full potential.

What does this mean in practice?

Let's say you're an individual seller who has a few products that sell pretty well. You're seeing consistent growth on Amazon and you're starting to make a name for yourself.

"Awesome," you think. "Maybe it's time for me to go to Amazon and buy more storage space so I can stock more products and prepare for growth."

That may not be able to happen!

At the time of writing, Amazon limits individual selling accounts to 10 cubic feet of space in a Fulfilment Centre.

That's it!

The value doesn't change unless Amazon says it changes, no matter how successful your products might be. And that means you can't even go to Amazon and buy more space in their warehouses as an individual seller. If you need more than 10 cubic feet, you're not getting it until Amazon decides you can have it!

Even professional selling accounts aren't immune to these types of limitations.

If you don't maintain an Inventory Performance Index (IPI) for your stock, Amazon may create a storage limit for you! It bases its decision on several factors, including:

- Available capacity in its Fulfilment Centres

- Your sales volume

- Any historical IPI scores you may have available

Now, these restrictions came into place as a result of the global pandemic. Amazon didn't want people using its Fulfilment Centres to stockpile products. They wanted whatever went into the centres to go back out of them as quickly as possible.

But guess what...

The pandemic isn't going to last forever!

While these storage limitations are frustrating in the short-term, they are a temporary measure. Remember that Amazon has undergone an unprecedented period of growth alongside the issues the pandemic causes.

That means it's investing heavily in new infrastructure, and new warehouses, as we speak!

So, don't worry too much about storage limitations if you're an Amazon seller. Eventually, they're going to ease. Who knows? By the time you read this book, FBA storage may not even be an issue anymore.

Challenge #4: Potential New Restrictions That Amazon May Introduce

So, we can see there are restrictions in place on storage space if you're using FBA.

The good news is that those restrictions are likely to be temporary. As Amazon works to create more Fulfilment Centres, it will eventually manage to strike a better balance between available storage space and the number of sellers that it services.

However, storage space isn't the only potential restriction you may face with physical products.

Have you heard of the Oberdorf v. Amazon court case in the United States? I hadn't until I started researching for this book!

Heather Oberdorf used Amazon to find a dog leash for her little puppy. She bought the leash from an independent seller using Amazon as their sales platform.

Heather received the product and everything seemed fine...

One day, Heather took her dog for a walk using the leash that she'd bought.

The leash snapped so violently as her dog pulled at it, it struck her in the face and almost blinded her in one eye!

Naturally, Heather wanted to sue the maker of the product.

The problem was that the seller was unreachable.

In the past, this would have been the end of the story. Amazon was just the platform the seller used so it couldn't be held liable for the defective product.

But not anymore!

Heather pursued Amazon for damages and courts in the United States decided that Amazon could be held responsible for the defective product.

That's huge!

It creates the possibility that Amazon could face more lawsuits as a result of dodgy sellers using the platform.

Do you think Amazon will just take that lying down?

Of course they won't!

The odds are that the outcome of this case will lead to Amazon implementing more restrictions than ever before on third-party sellers. After all, the company has to protect itself.

Still, more restrictions mean a harder time for third-party sellers. But!

And this is a but that's so big that it would wow Sir Mix-A-Lot...

Nothing's happened yet! All of this is just speculation on my part about the reaction that Amazon might have to such cases.

It's also entirely possible that it will continue to fight these issues in court so it gets a more favourable ruling.

But even if more stringent restrictions do come into place, that's not going to affect you as a seller. After all, sourcing and selling quality products is what you do, so you don't have to worry about liability issues.

Challenge #5: The Fees Associated With Selling on Amazon

It costs money to sell on Amazon.

There's no way around that.

If you're using FBA, you have to pay fees that vary depending on the amount of space your products take up. Even if you don't use FBA, you've still got to spend money on warehousing and delivery yourself.

But let's take the logistics out of the equation.

Amazon still charges you for using the platform.

At the time of writing, it costs $49.95 to sign up for the company's Professional Plan. On top of that, you may have to pay additional selling fees, such as referral fees and closing fees.

"Okay," you think. "I'll just go for the Individual plan."

That might work.

The Individual plan doesn't come with a monthly subscription. However, you will get charged $0.99 for every sale that you make. And that's before any additional fees get taken into account! If you make more than 50 sales in a month, you end up paying more than you would for the Professional plan!

My point?

You have to spend money to make money on Amazon.

Again, the sums here aren't huge by any means. And in most cases, it only takes a few sales of your product to pay the monthly fee and move into the pure profit zone.

Still, such fees can be a little prohibitive if you're starting out with very little money in your bank account.

But that's okay too.

Why?

The model I'm going to introduce you to in this book costs even less than setting up an Amazon store. So, if you're not in a position to sell physical products on Amazon right now, you can sell something else instead. And once you've built that other business, you can use the profits you generate to set up your physical product store when you're in a more comfortable position!

Selling Products Isn't the Only Way to Create an Income Using Amazon

Wow! That sounded like an awful lot of doom and gloom there, didn't it? So, let me get something straight...

Selling physical products on Amazon will always be a viable way to create a passive income. It's what I teach, it's what I've mastered, and it's something I encourage as a stream of income.

All I'm saying is that it's a touch harder to sell physical products on Amazon right now because of the complications the pandemic created.

But here's the good news...

First, those complications are all temporary, which means they're not going to be around for long.

Second, even if you face some of these challenges, there's no reason why you can't overcome them. As long as you know what you're doing with your Amazon store, you may never even have to deal with them.

And finally, there's a new way to use Amazon to create a passive income stream!

If you're not comfortable setting up a physical product store right now, this new model is for you.

If you already have an Amazon store and want to make even more money through the platform, this model is definitely for you!

Ready to find out what it is?

I reveal all in the next chapter.

Chapter Three

Introducing the New Opportunity – Amazon Kindle!

He'd finally made it. After years of writing, rewriting, and exploring every idea that came into his head, Mark Dawson had landed a publishing deal.

His book, *The Art of Falling Apart*, would be published by Pan Books in 2000. The release date loomed nearer and Mark continued tweaking the book. Tightening plot threads...

Snipping the loose ends...

By the time it was published, Mark felt confident that he had a great book to offer to his audience. The release date came and went, with Mark awaiting the sales figures.

His jaw dropped when he received them.

The Art of Falling Apart bombed spectacularly.

Practically nobody bought it and the book soon ended up lost in the ether alongside so many other novels that fail to catch fire with an audience.

For a good while afterwards, Mark turned over the possible reasons for the failure in his head.

Was the book no good?

He certainly didn't feel that way as he wrote it. He'd worked so hard on creating something riveting that the possibility of people thinking it was poorly-written hadn't crossed his mind.

No, the quality wasn't the issue here. It was marketing.

Mark's book didn't sell because few people were even aware that it existed. And the blame for that problem lay at the feet of his publishers. After all, it was their job to get people excited about the book. It was their job to publicise this new release.

And they'd clearly done a crappy job.

It was around this time that Mark made a decision that changed his life. If his publishers couldn't do their job properly, he'd do it for them.

And so started Mark Dawson's adventures into the world of self-publishing.

Mark discovered Amazon Kindle Direct Publishing and decided to launch his second book on the platform.

And then his third... And his fourth...

I won't go into all of the tactics that Mark used to make sure these books got in front of a wider audience. All you need to know is that they did.

And the profits?

In 2015 alone, Mark Dawson made over $450,000 from his books thanks to Amazon Kindle.

And as a prolific author, that six-figure income has surely only increased in the years that followed.

"Hold on a second," I hear you say... "Why are you suddenly talking to me about an author?"

It's simple...

Amazon Kindle is the amazing new online selling opportunity that I've been hinting at all of this time. With Kindle, you have the opportunity to leverage your expertise and knowledge to create books that are available to buyers 24/7!

I'm going to get into how you'll do that in later chapters.

10 Reasons why Selling on Kindle is a Great Idea

First, I want you to get crystal clear on why selling on Kindle is such a great idea. And thanks to my own experience of developing this revenue stream, I can come up with 10 right off the top of my head.

Reason #1: You Pay No Shipping Costs For Digital Books

I explained all of this earlier, but add all of the money you're paying for shipping, storage, and Amazon itself and you have a whole bunch of fees to deal with.

But as a Kindle publisher, a bunch of those fees go right out of the window!

Shipping? You don't need to ship something that can be downloaded!

Storage? You don't need to store something that isn't a physical product!

The point is that publishing books via Kindle Direct Publishing costs a lot less than selling a physical product, regardless of how you choose to sell.

You just need to write the book and get it online!

Reason #2: You Need Less Help Running a Kindle Business

When you start your Amazon business, you can do a lot of it on your own.

Maybe you can store products in the garage. If you're really diligent, you might even send orders out yourself.

That will work for a short while.

But eventually, you're going to want to grow the business. And that always means bringing people on board to help you run things. This includes hiring external services, which is what you do when you pay for warehouse space or sign a contract with a transportation company.

However, this often also means building an internal team.

For example, an Amazon business that has several products on the move will almost certainly need an Operations Manager. You'll want to have somebody in place to keep all of your balls in the air. After all, doing it all yourself defeats the purpose of creating a business that offers you freedom!

A growing Amazon business has several moving parts. And that isn't a bad thing. If you're at the point where you need to build a team to sell an Amazon, that means you're doing a really good job at selling on Amazon.

Awesome work.

But if you don't quite feel ready to manage a team then guess what? You won't need to build one for a Kindle business!

You're not dealing with physical inventory, which means no messing around with warehouses and logistics. You also only have one product. Once a book's published, it doesn't need any changes unless you choose to make some tweaks. Compare that to physical products, which you have to ensure are of a certain quality before you sell them, and you have a business that's a lot easier to run.

And if it's easier to run, that means you don't need a large team to run it!

In fact, it's very possible to run a lucrative Kindle business on your own. And that means you get to make a bigger profit because you have fewer expenses to deal with.

Reason #3: There's More Demand Than Ever

Since COVID hit, eBook sales have rocketed up by 60%. By the end of 2020, the eBook industry generated $16.6 billion.

And just so you know, nine out of every 10 eBook sales take place on the Kindle platform.

The point? There's more demand for eBooks than there has ever been before. And it makes sense. After all, we have millions of people stuck in lockdown with nothing to do.

They're spending more time on Netflix... They're spending more time on computer games...

And a lot of them are spending more time curled up with a good book!

If you can start publishing eBooks now, you're doing so in an environment that's tailor-made for you to succeed. The demand is already there. All you have to do is create some books that cater to the demand.

Reason #4: Kindle Helps People Declutter

I'm going to assume that you enjoy a good book... I'm also going to assume that you have a bookshelf at home...

Have you ever taken a close look at that thing? I bet it's already full to the brim with books and you still want to buy more. That is a problem that millions of other avid readers have!

Physical books take up a ton of space. They also create all sorts of environmental issues. After all, a physical book requires paper, which means a tree is getting chopped down somewhere to make it. Think about all of the millions of physical books in the world and that's a lot of dead trees.

Kindle provides a solution to all of those problems.

Having all of their books on a single device means that your customers don't have to clutter up the house with tons of physical books. And better yet, selling on Kindle means you appeal to the environmentally conscious.

They don't have to worry about where the paper's coming from when there's no paper involved!

Reason #5: Books Help You Build Authority

"Hi. My name's Sophie Howard and I'm the author of…"

Let's stop right there and take a look at the word "author".

How good does that sound when you hear it? When I saw I'm the author of something, you instantly assume that I know what I'm talking about, right? After all, I wrote the book on it!

That is one of the secret powers of a good book.

If you've written something that people want to read, you gain instant authority. Beyond any money that you earn from it, the book becomes a tool that you can use to establish yourself as an expert in your niche.

Let's say you're a coach who's selling a course.

That's another great way to use the web to create a revenue stream.

And if you've written and published a book, you now have something that you can use to showcase your expertise in your chosen niche. People can read the book, see what you're all about and, if they like it, pay money to work with you.

The revenue you generate from a book doesn't necessarily only come from the sale of the book itself. That book could also lead to people buying more of what you're selling because it establishes you as an authority.

Reason #6: Fewer Compliance Issues

I think I made my point about compliance issues in the last chapter…

When you're selling products, you have a lot of rules to follow. And that goes beyond whatever regulations Amazon has (and might have in the future). For example, if you're in the States and you're selling a food item or a supplement, you've got the FDA telling you that you need to have a list of approved ingredients on the package.

What if one of your ingredients isn't FDA-approved? Boom! The product's gone.

With products, you also have manufacturing standards to meet. If your product runs on electricity, you have to meet electrical standards in all of the countries that you want to sell in.

These challenges are part and parcel of running an Amazon store. And again, they're certainly not things that should stop you from selling physical products. As long as you understand the compliance issues that relate to your product, you can ensure anything you sell meets the requirements!

Still, compliance can be a bit of a headache... And it's a headache that you get to avoid if you decide to sell on Kindle instead.

An eBook doesn't need an ingredient list. It doesn't need manufacturer oversight. It just needs a good topic, a strong audience, and the right platform to launch it on.

Reason #7: You Don't Need to Be a Techie

This all sounds great, right?

But I know that you have a big concern floating around in your head...

To make this work, surely you have to be a techie? You have to know your way around computers and know how to design your book. Maybe that means learning how to code? Surely it means spending a whole lot of time in front of the computer learning how this whole thing works.

Not really!

Amazon has worked hard to make Kindle Direct Publishing as user-friendly as possible. That means you're not going to spend hours trying to figure out how the platform works. In most cases, you can just follow the instructions the platform gives you and you'll have your book online in no time.

And that brings me to my next point...

Reason #8: You Can Upload a Book and Start Selling It the Same Day

It can take a couple of months to get a product ready to go on Amazon. And even once you've launched, you have to keep track of stock to make sure you're selling at the level you should be.

All very manageable, of course. Still, the process of getting a product onto Amazon does take a little bit of time.

But with an eBook? Once you've written the thing, you can upload it and start selling it on the same day. There's no waiting around for approval. There's no back and forth with manufacturers. Once it's ready to go, it's good to go!

And that means you can start making money from the moment that you finish your book.

Reason #9: You Can React to the Market

The ease of putting a book up for sale doesn't only mean that you get money coming in faster. It also means you have a market advantage.

When the market changes, you have the ability to self-publish a book in a matter of weeks, or days if you're quick enough.

For example, you might notice that there's a trend towards books about Tarot reading that you want to jump onto.

With Kindle publishing, the only thing you need to do is get the book written.

You can react to this trend in the market almost instantly, which means you get to catch the trend at its peak rather than having to wait and potentially jumping onto it when it's already on the way down.

Reason #10: You Don't Have to Write the Books Yourself

I'm sure you can see just how much of an opportunity Kindle publishing offers. There's just one problem... You've never written a book in your life.

And if you're honest with yourself, you're not much of a writer in the first place. All of the speed advantages in the world don't mean anything if you have to spend a huge amount of time learning how to write!

Who said anything about you being the person who writes the books that you publish?

There are plenty of ghost-writing agencies that can do the hard work for you.

In a lot of cases, they just need to know what you want to write about and they'll handle everything else.

Research...

Structure...

Putting the whole thing together...

A good agency can do it all! That means all you need to do is send the instructions, check the final result, and get it uploaded!

There's a Huge Opportunity Here for You

And I bet it's an opportunity that you never saw coming.

Most people don't think of books as a potential income stream. They see authors as people who pour years of their lives into writing just one book that might not even sell.

But Kindle changed all of that.

With Kindle Direct Publishing, you have the opportunity to create a brand-new revenue stream that could potentially generate a new income for you.

Chapter Four

How I Went From $0 to Six Figures With Kindle Direct Publishing (In Less Than Six Months!)

My career was going pretty well. I'd worked my way up through the New Zealand government, eventually ascending to the role of diplomat. I made decent money and, for a time, I was pretty happy in my work.

But my life was about to change.

I received the news that I was pregnant with my first child.

I can't describe the overwhelming sense of joy that I experienced when I discovered that I was preparing to bring a new life into the world. But those emotions were soon overwhelmed with feelings of doubt...

I worked in a career that placed enormous demands on my time. When I was only responsible for myself, this wasn't much of an issue. I could justify dedicating so much of myself to my work, especially as my husband was so supportive.

But now, I'd have a little one to take care of...

And my job as a diplomat just wasn't going to cut it anymore. I needed something that offered me more freedom, both financially and in terms of how I lived my life.

I needed something that would allow me to be a constant presence in the life of my child.

I needed Amazon... I just didn't know it yet.

I grappled with these feelings while still doing my job to the best of my abilities. And before I knew it, the happy day came.

I was a mother. And I went on maternity leave.

With a little time on my hands (and I mean a little as any mother will tell you that taking care of a newborn is a full-time job), I started doing some research. I knew that I needed a career change but I wasn't quite sure what that would look like.

Time and again, I kept landing on the same idea... Start an Amazon store. So... I did. And 18 months later, I had a store that I was able to sell for a cool 7 figures USD. I'd found the answer and it was Amazon.

I won't bore you with all of the details of my career in the years since that sale. Needless to say, I left my government role almost as soon as I saw the potential that Amazon offered.

And today, I specialise in helping people who are in the position I was in...

Feeling stuck... Wanting a change... And with a burning desire to create the life of their dreams...

I teach these people how to build powerful Amazon stores that act as the key to their freedom kingdoms.

My name is Sophie Howard.

And I teach people how to succeed on Amazon.

The New Idea

Now, I could have stuck solely with my Amazon businesses and happily succeeded with those.

But that just isn't in my nature.

As passionate as I am about finding new products that audiences love, I'm also passionate about creating the best possible life for myself and my family. And I learned long ago that the best way to do that is to create multiple streams of revenue.

Why?

Having multiple streams of revenue protects you. If something goes wrong in one area, you still have several other streams coming in to support you.

It also accelerates you towards your goals.

For example, if having one stream of income allows me to pay off my house in 30 years, having two may shorten that time to 15 years.

Having three may shorten it to 10 years.

You get the picture.

My point is that I'm always on the lookout for new ways to generate revenue.

What I didn't expect was that I'd find a new and powerful revenue stream on the very platform that I specialise in!

eBooks.

I'd never given them much thought before.

Sure, I'd written a few to demonstrate my expertise as an Amazon seller. But those books were all about building my authority.

I was an author. I poured everything I had into those books.

But that wasn't conducive to a book-based business model. The books just served as a way of supporting my main business. There wasn't a revenue-generating machine there so I didn't focus on books at all.

That was until I realised that taking a different approach might just work.

What if I wasn't an author... What if my model acted more like a publishing business?

What if I outsourced the creation of the content and focused solely on uploading the books and generating a profit from them. I wouldn't need staff. I wouldn't even need to write. All I'd have to do is come up with the ideas, find the right people to bring the books to life, and then publish those books via Kindle Direct Publishing.

I started running some numbers in my head.

Let's say we do a book or two per month. Say...20 books per year. That's very doable! We're not writing huge novels here, after all.

Now, each of those books will cost between $500 and $1,000 to produce. So, if we go at the top end, that means 20 books will cost me $20,000.

That's a good chunk of cash!

But it's more than worth it if the returns are high enough. And if each of those books manages to sell enough copies to generate between $1,000 and $2,000 in revenue per month, I'd have a six-figure business model before I knew it!

And everything I'd have to do would be a one-time thing!

One time coming up with the idea and plan behind the book... One time briefing the writer... One time paying that writer a few hundred dollars to create the book...

One time uploading it to Amazon.

The idea for this new business model took shape in my head. Soon, I started focusing less on the potential outcome and more on the challenges that I'd need to overcome.

I'd need to carry out great keyword research.

I'd need to find good ghost-writing agencies to outsource the book ideas too. And I'd need to come up with book ideas that could sell.

All challenges...

All eminently surmountable!

I'd sold myself on the idea. And soon enough, I had a model in place to bring the idea to life!

My Results

At the time of writing, I'm about three years down the line from when I first launched my book publishing model.

And I have to say I've achieved amazing results faster than even I anticipated!

I went into this thing thinking that getting 20 books online would be a good achievement. But now, I have dozens of books available on Kindle in a little over two years. I found the right people to handle the writing work and finding subjects to write about was easier than I thought it would be.

And as for the writing?

I haven't done a word of it!

Outside of the couple of books that I'd already written, all 40 of these books were ghost-written by agencies that I'm working with.

None of these new books are published under my name. They all have anonymous authors. We basically invent a writer and build a brand around them for each of the different topics that we focus on.

We even have ghostwriters from other countries writing books in Italian, Spanish, and French for us! That means we get to sell out books all over the world!

Sounds great, right?

The books that I've already published will continue to sell. The books that I have in the pipeline will add to what I already have.

This Kindle Direct Publishing thing isn't going to be a six-figure business for me, it could even by a 7 figure business.

Combining physical products with Kindle eBooks has put me in a stronger financial position than I've ever been in before. And that means I have complete and utter freedom to do whatever I want with my life!

Are You Ready to Write Your Own Success Story?

So, I've proven to myself that my Kindle Direct Publishing Model works. You can see the numbers staring back at you from the page too. Now, here's what I want you to understand...

This could be you! There is nothing that I've done that you couldn't do.

This model doesn't require you to be an outstanding writer. It doesn't require you to spend years of your life massaging an idea until you turn it into a book. And it certainly doesn't require you to deal with difficult tech.

The model is simple... It's elegant... And it's something that you can set up today to create a part time online business with the potential hat changes your life forever!

Are you ready to learn more?

We're going to spend the rest of this book diving into the mechanics behind the model. Get this right and you'll create your own money-making machine!

Chapter Five

The Kindle Basics. And How to Select a Topic to Write About

Several years... That's how long the half-written first draft for a book entitled Emperor's Edge sat on Lindsay Buroker's computer.

Sure, she thought she'd finish it eventually.

But life always seemed to manage to get in the way.

Like so many potential authors, she just had a half-baked idea that could be something great if she just dedicated herself to it.

Unlike many potential authors...she managed to complete her book!

After reading about a few people who'd enjoyed success through self-publishing, she decided to sit down and get the thing written. She thought the end result was pretty good.

But she didn't want to have to go through the potential heartbreak of sending the book off to literary agents only for them to reject her.

She didn't want to deal with publishers either.

Her book didn't quite fit into the little niches that publishers like to place books into.

So, she turned to Kindle Direct Publishing.

Having bought a Kindle herself a couple of years prior, she knew that it was a great source of books. But it was only after researching the platform herself that she discovered just how easy it would be to use it to launch her own novel.

That's exactly what she did.

Within a couple of months, she was making four-figure royalties from sales of her first book.

And that was all of the encouragement she needed.

Over the course of a year, she knocked out another three books and suddenly had an Amazon publishing business on her hands!

Her old job?

Gone!

She didn't need it anymore.

Writing and publishing became her full-time occupation, which meant she got to stay home and enjoy her life on her terms.

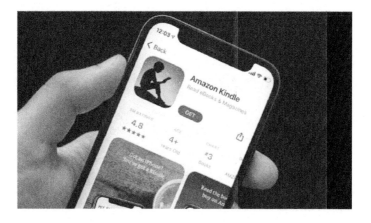

Getting Set Up on Kindle – The Six Steps

Of course, Lindsay's model is a little different from the one that I'm going to teach you. She's an author and writes all of her books herself.

You're likely not going to do that.

What you are going to do is get yourself set up on Kindle Direct Publishing so that you can start pumping out books and making a profit from them. But before you can put our model into practice, you've got to handle the basics first.

You've got to get set up on Kindle!

The good news is that it's just a case of following a few simple steps:

Step #1: Create Your Kindle Publishing Account

Setting up a Kindle Direct Publishing account is easier than you might think.

All you need to do is jump onto Amazon and scroll right to the bottom of the page. In the footer, you should see a little category called "Make Money with Us". Near the bottom of the list, you'll see a link that says "Self-Publish with Us":

Click on that link and you're taken to a page that tells you some of the benefits of Kindle Direct Publishing and encourages you to sign in if you haven't already.

Once you sign in, you just have to accept Amazon's terms and handle whatever adjustments or additions it asks you to make to your profile.

Congratulations!

You're officially signed up to Kindle Direct Publishing!

See how easy that was?

All that's left is to get your first book online!

Step #2: Create a Title

Once you've registered an account, Amazon will take you to your very own Kindle dashboard. It's here that you'll track and manage all of the books that you publish.

The full page is a little longer than this.

Amazon prompts you to fill out all of the basic details for your book. You can see in the screenshot that it asks for the Language, Book Title, and whether your book is part of a Series.

Keep scrolling down and Amazon will prompt you to enter an Edition Number, an Author, any Contributors, and a Description.

Fill everything out and keep scrolling down the form until you get to...

Keywords   Enter up to 7 search keywords that describe your book. How do I choose keywords?

                  Your Keywords (Optional)

Step #3: Enter Your Keywords

Amazon allows you to enter seven keywords for your book, as you can see here:

The keywords are words that you anticipate a potential reader using to find a book in your niche. That means you've got to be very careful with your keyword selection. Go too broad and you risk your book getting lost in a sea of competitors. Go too narrow and the keyword may be so specific that nobody searches for it.

How do you find appropriate keywords? I'm going to tell you a little later on!

Step #4: Set Your Categories

Once you've chosen your keywords, it's time to select the appropriate categories for your book.

Amazon allows you to pick two and there are hundreds to choose from.

Again, accuracy is key here. Your book categories have to directly relate to the content of your book. They also need to be categories that are popular enough for you to achieve sales through them.

You'll generally come up with your categories when you choose a topic to write about. I won't tell you how to do that here because I'm going to cover it in much more depth later on in this very chapter!

Step #5: Upload the Book

After filling out a couple more details about your book, you're ready to upload!

There are two elements to this:

- Uploading a cover.

- Uploading the book content.

Let's start with the cover.

Now, Amazon doesn't actually require you to have a cover in place for your book. You can launch without one, though I don't recommend it. Without a cover, your book looks unprofessional, which means readers are less likely to click on it!

This is one of the more difficult aspects of getting a book online because Amazon has a ton of specifications for your cover design. I won't go into them here because you can find them all at this link - https://kdp.amazon.com/en_US/help/topic/ G200645690

My advice? Get someone else to do it!

There are plenty of freelancers on sites like Upwork and Freelanc er.com who specialise in Amazon cover design.

Give them an idea of what you want and make sure that they understand the specifications that Amazon makes them follow.

Have somebody design the cover for you and all you have to do is upload the image!

After that, you just need to upload the book content.

This is much simpler.

Before you upload, Amazon will ask if you want to add Digital Rights Management (DRM) to your book. The idea behind this is that the DRM will make it harder for people to steal the content and use it for their own purposes.

Sounds great, right?

The downside is that it also makes it more difficult for your readers to enjoy your book the way they want to. For example, DRM may prevent the reader from reading your book on a non-Kindle device.

So, when you have it active, you create a barrier.

We want reading your book to be a simple process for your audience, so it's probably best to go without DRM. After all, the odds of somebody stealing your book (and you not knowing about it) are pretty slim.

Once you made the DRM choice, all that's left is to upload the book's content. Amazon accepts files in the following formats:

- PDF

- Word (Both .doc and .docx files)

- Text

- ePub

- HTML

Just choose the file and click the button to upload it.

Awesome!

You're almost done. We just have one last step to run through...

Step #6: Preview the Book

Never publish your eBook without previewing it first!

As great a job as Amazon does of automatically formatting your content, it doesn't get it right 100% of the time. Sometimes, the formatting will go wonky. You might end up with images in the wrong places or text that doesn't line up properly.

If you publish your book in that state, it looks unprofessional.

That decreases the book's authority...

And ultimately, it leads to fewer sales than you deserve!

So, preview the book and make any formatting changes you need to make. Amazon allows you to preview how the book will look on multiple devices.

Take advantage of that to ensure you're providing a consistent experience to your readers!

Once you've handled all of that (it gets easier with time as you work out what issues could lead to poor formatting) you're ready to publish.

One click of a button and your book is released into the world!

Choosing a Topic to Write About

So...we know how to upload a book to Amazon.

That's the easy part. Before you can follow the steps I've just shared, you need to have a book to publish.

Now, I've already skimmed through some of the steps for creating that book. You know that you're going to work with external agencies who can come up with the copy, the cover, etc.

But even before any of that, you need to come up with an appropriate subject.

And when I say "appropriate", I don't necessarily mean a subject that you're passionate about. Passion can only take you so far if that passion lies in a subject that people aren't interested in!

The art of choosing a good book subject lies in research.

It's about discovering what people want to read about and providing them with the perfect book for their needs.

If the subject's too obscure, it's not going to be popular enough to generate a profit.

If the subject's too obvious, a million and one writers will have already covered it. Your job is to find a subject that's popular enough while having low competition.

And in this sense, choosing a book topic is much like choosing a product to sell on Amazon. It's not about jumping into a category that already has tons of books and a huge audience.

It's about finding a niche that perhaps isn't served as well as it could be and providing a product that suits the niche.

Only in this case, the product is your book!

To add to this, the goal is also to have a book that's capable of generating revenue for years to come. That means avoiding subjects that will likely be short-lived or seasonal. They may generate a profit for a little while but they'll eventually die off and do nothing for your new Kindle business!

The Research Tool That You Can't Do Without

So, we know you want to write about a niche topic that offers enough demand and low competition.

The question now is how do you find that topic.

Simple!

I use a great research tool that tells me everything that I need to know about any topic that I'm thinking about publishing a book on.

And though that price may vary a little, depending on what offers the company has in place, the fact is that this one-time outlay will get repaid many times over once you start selling books!

Let's say you've got your hands on the tool. It has a 60-day trial by the way, so there's no excuse not to try it!

So, how do I use KDSpy?

Let's say that I think a book about potty training might be a possibility for my publishing business.

I boot up KDSpy and I use it to research books in the "Potty Training" category.

I see that the top-selling book generates about $60,000 in revenue per month. The second book on the list generates $27,000 and the third one generates £18,000 per month.

Those are great numbers for the people who've published those books.

The problem is that they're a little too big for me! I look at those numbers and see that there's clearly plenty of demand for books on this subject. However, I can also see that the books that are already out there do a great job of servicing that demand.

If I try and add to that, I've got to break the stranglehold that these top three books have on the niche.

And frankly, I don't think that's going to happen. And even if it did, it would only happen because I spent a ton of time and money on promoting the book.

That's not what I want to do so the potty-training idea is out of the question. See how it works?

If there's high competition, you want to avoid the category.

Now, how about we start looking at a couple of categories that would make for good choices?

How about a cookbook?

Now. I already know what you're thinking...

There are millions of cookbooks out there! How could this possibly be a good area to go into when there are full-blown celebrities to compete with?

Simple!

It all depends on the niche you target.

For example, let's say I type "*Gastric Sleeve Bariatric Cookbook*" into KDSpy.

That's a super-niche topic but I know that it has an audience. According to the American Society for Metabolic and Bariatric Surgery, 228,000 bariatric procedures were performed in 2017 in the US alone.

Go global from there and you probably have close to half a million people per year undergoing this type of surgery.

That's a pretty big audience.

And every one of those people will need advice. They're going to have to change their entire diets so a cookbook that's safe for them might be just what they need.

Seems like a good idea.

So, I type it into KDSpy…

The top-selling book that matches this keyword makes $20,000 per month. The books below it may make a couple of thousand dollars.

Those are good numbers for me.

The competition's low enough for this specific type of cookbook to be successful, as long as I do it well. And the topic has an audience that isn't going to run out (people have gastric bypass surgery every year).

Perfect!

This is the sort of topic that I'd go for.

And that, in a nutshell, shows you how to choose a topic to write about.

You're not chasing your passions here. You're not writing about things that you're the expert in. Instead, you're finding topics for which a demand exists that isn't being served as well as it could be.

KDSpy will help you to run the numbers.

And once you've found the right topic, you just need to make sure you can create the right book and build a strong model around it!

You're All Set Up!

You have your Kindle account... You know how to find suitable topics for your books...

Now, it's time to launch the model. It's time to get some books written and get them published in the right way so that they generate thousands of dollars in revenue every month for you.

And the best part about this model?

Once you have a book up and running, you never have to touch it again. For as long as it's available, it will generate revenue for you. And every book you publish afterwards will follow the same routine. Get it done, get it online, and wait for the cash to roll in.

How good does that sound?

With Kindle Direct Publishing, you can create a passive income stream that will provide you with true freedom. You'll never have to trade your time for money again because you'll get everything you need from your books.

So...how about we look a little closer at the model you need to deploy?

FREE WORKSHOP:

Your Kindle eBook Business Made Easy

As a reader of my book, you're clearly someone that takes self-education seriously.

And, that's a wise move – because as Tony Robbins mentor Jim Rohn said:

"Formal education can make you a living. Self- Education can make you a fortune."

It's true – the more you learn, the more you can earn.

Discover how to set up a new potential income stream selling eBooks on Amazon Kindle as quickly and easily as possible.

CLICK HERE TO SECURE YOUR FREE SPOT

Or scan the QR Code

Chapter Six

The Kindle Income Stream Model

Wynne Channing already had an established career as a business journalist. She was published... She could certainly write...

And she just so happened to have a passion for vampires that led her down the novelist route. After working for a while, she produced a "Young Adult" book called *What Kills Me*.

She felt pretty confident that a publisher would want in.

At the time, books about vampires were all of the rage, especially with teenagers. And with her journalistic pedigree backing her up, Wynne knew that she had the tools to write a great novel.

Feeling quietly confident, she shipped the manuscript out to 20 different publishers and awaited their replies.

Perhaps she had visions of igniting a bidding war floating around in her head...

Unfortunately, any idea of that happening came crashing down to Earth when reality bit her. The vast majority of the 20 publishers didn't even bother to respond to her.

The few that did contact her said that they weren't interested in the topic and hadn't even bothered to read the manuscript!

The blow almost crushed her. Wynne almost gave up on her hopes of publishing the book. But one day, she had a fateful conversation with a friend who revealed another option...

Kindle Direct Publishing.

Wynne could publish the book herself through Amazon and let it stand on its own merits. If it didn't sell then fair enough. The publishers were right and she'd know for sure that this book wasn't as good as she'd hoped.

But if it did sell... The possibilities were endless!

Wynne uploaded the book with a $2.99 price tag and nothing happened. "Okay," she thought. "I guess I'll lower the price."

She dropped it down to $0.99 and the book took off. It flew into Amazon's bestseller list for the "Occult" and the "Action and Adventure" categories. Suddenly, people wanted to talk to Wynne about her book.

She got great reviews... She appeared in interviews...

And the book, even though it was only priced at $0.99, made a ton of money!

Wynne's story shows us just what can happen if you publish the right book, at the right time, and to the right niche.

Are you ready to achieve a similar level of success without having to write a word?

Let's build your publishing model!

Building Your Model — The Things You Need to Know

I get it...

You're a little scared about publishing on Kindle because you think it's going to take a ton of time and effort. Even though you're not writing the books, you still don't know how to succeed on the platform.

What if you publish a bunch of books and get nothing to show for it? It could happen...

But it won't because I'm going to share the exact model that I used to make a six figure monthly income through Kindle Direct Publishing!

After working through the last chapter, you have an account and you know how to find a suitable topic. Now that you know what the book is going to be about, follow these steps to craft your publishing model.

Step #1: Have an Agency Handle the Writing for You

I've touched on this already but it's worth repeating here...

You don't have to write a single word of the books that you publish.

You're not the author here. In this model, you're the branding specialist who comes up with the ideas and publishes the books in such a way that they're sure to sell.

And this is great news for you because writing is the hardest part of the whole process!

There are tons of copywriting and ghostwriting agencies out there who can handle these types of projects. There are also a whole bunch of freelancers who are just itching to dig their claws into writing a good book. There's a whole world of people out there who have creative writing or English Literature degrees. They read all day and write whenever they get the chance.

They love doing this stuff!

So...let them do it!

How do you find the right people for the job?

Here are a couple of quick tips based on my own experiences:

- **Look for people who have experience writing books for the Kindle platform.** That experience means they should know everything about correct formatting, which means they're less likely to make silly mistakes.

- **Do your research into any agency or writer that you consider working with.** In particular, look out for allegations of plagiarism on their part. There are tons of online tools that scan for plagiarism and it only takes one valid accusation to take your book down. And when that happens, you get in trouble with Amazon and anger whoever published the content your writer copied.

- **Always ask for samples from the writer who will work on your project.** I wasted a lot of time trying to find good writers during the early days of launching this model. It's better to get somebody good from the start than to forge ahead while hoping the writer's up to the task.

Step #2: Make Sure Each Book Suits Kindle, Paperback and Audiobook

It goes without saying that you need to make sure your book suits the Kindle format.

That's your main publishing platform and Amazon gives you every tool that you need to make this happen.

But I also want to make it clear that Kindle isn't the only platform that you can use to make money from your books.

You have the option of the more traditional route too. If one of your books takes off on Kindle, launching a paperback version may be a possibility. After all, there are plenty of people who prefer reading real books instead of reading on an electronic device. If you strike gold, publishing a paperback version may help you to mine a little more out of your audience.

And then, we come to audiobooks.

This is such an underserved area of the book market.

It costs about $200 to $300 to hire somebody to narrate your book for you. Once you have that recording, you can jump on Audible and upload it there.

Voila!

Now, you have your eBook available in another format and can potentially double the revenue that it generates. And Audible is the perfect platform to use because it's also owned by Amazon.

That means it's familiar and you know that it's going to reach the widest audience possible!

My point is that your eBook is just the start.

Kindle is just one of several potential revenue streams you can create using that book. Releasing a paperback version creates another stream. And creating an audiobook gives you even more.

Step #3: Use Keyword Research Software to Find Out What People Are Searching For

I've already touched on this when I talked about choosing a topic.

Research is your friend when it comes to knowing what to write about. That's where the keyword research tool comes in. The tool shows you what the numbers look like so you can choose the correct niche.

But that's not all it shows you!

It also offers you some insight into the keywords that readers use to access titles in your chosen niche!

Remember when I walked you through setting up your Kindle account and publishing your first book online? There was a section about keywords in that guide. You have the ability to choose seven keywords that you think people will use to search for your book.

Don't make your choices based on intuition.

Don't imagine what you might search for and go with those keywords.

Instead, use tools like KDSpy to get real numbers so you know exactly which keywords to target.

Of course, KDSpy isn't the only tool that can help you do this. I like using Publisher Rocket as it also provides you with a keyword list that you can use to ensure your books reach the right people. You can find that tool here - https://publisherrocket.com

Combine the lists that each tool gives you and pick the seven that offer the best results.

And remember...

You need to do this for every book you publish!

Step #4: Aim to Create a Book per Month

Earlier, I told you that I created 40 books within six months. That's a rate of about six or seven books per month.

Now, I hit those numbers for two reasons...

First, I wanted to test my model as thoroughly as I could before I presented it to other people. As such, I accelerated my book production so that I could confirm that this worked the way I thought it would. With 40 books, I reached six figures per month.

Second, I already had a lot of infrastructure in place. I knew how Amazon and Kindle worked. I already have a lot of content created for me, which meant I knew where to look to find good writers.

And finally, I'm in a position where I can make a couple of mistakes along the way and not have them affect me financially or otherwise.

My guess is that you're not in the same position right now. And that's why I don't recommend shooting for 40 books in six months!

Instead, I recommend trying to publish one book per month.

Why?

Shooting for one book per month gives you plenty of time to find the right people to create the books. It also helps you get to grips with managing this type of operation and allows you to experiment with Kindle a little bit.

12 books per year is manageable while still offering enough frequency to make this a viable model for you.

Let's say those 12 books each ended up generating $5,000 per month in revenue. At the end of the year, that amounts to $60,000 per month... Recurring!

And then the next year, you can release another 12 books to get to $120,000. Or, you could accelerate your book production and really build this thing up.

Just keep it a little slower and a little steadier during the first year. Spend that year putting all of the pieces in place and then you can accelerate!

Step #5: Get Support From A Team That Can Help You Finally, Understand That You Don't Have To Do All Of This Alone.

In fact, I don't recommend that at all. As simple as the Kindle publishing model is, you're still creating a business in an area that you're probably not familiar with. Going it alone opens you up to making more mistakes than you really need to, which will slow down your progress.

Instead of doing that, get a little help from people who've been there and done it. People like me!

Your next step is to attend my free workshop to find out more!

FREE WORKSHOP:

Your Kindle eBook Business Made Easy

As a reader of my book, you're clearly someone that takes self-education seriously.

And, that's a wise move – because as Tony Robbins mentor Jim Rohn said:

"Formal education can make you a living. Self- Education can make you a fortune."

It's true – the more you learn, the more you can earn.

Discover how to set up a new potential income stream selling eBooks on Amazon Kindle as quickly and easily as possible.

CLICK HERE TO SECURE YOUR FREE SPOT

Or scan the QR Code

Hi, I'm Sophie Howard and if you want to learn how to earn passive income on Amazon with digital products – then you're in the right place.

I've written this book because after five years of being in business myself and running online businesses, I've seen a lot of different models and I've learned a lot of the different ways that lead to success.

I have also made mistakes and learned a lot of lessons along the way. What I now know to be true is that anyone can find their own path to financial freedom, but it won't be the same path for everyone. This book is for anyone who is seeking financial freedom and the path less travelled.

Read on to discover the path to fulfil your dreams and live the life you desire.

As I started raising my young family, priorities were changing. I realized that what I really wanted was more freedom. I resented all that wasted time and office politics.

I was partially motivated by the financial side, to generate a level of income that would allow me the quality of life I wanted to live.

But I also wanted to have other sorts of freedom, such as location independence. I wanted a business I could run from home. I wanted a business that didn't require full-time work.

I thought it must be possible to start something that lets me generate enough income to live really well, but live life on my terms.

Printed in Great Britain
by Amazon

28896088R00050